TEXAS

. . . in Historic Sites and Symbols

Drawings by Betsy Warren

1984 • HENDRICK-LONG PUBLISHING COMPANY • HOUSTON

Copyright 1982

ISBN 0-937460-05-2

FRIENDSHIP

State Motto

TEXAS is an Indian word.

It means *friends* or *allies*.

TEXAS FLAG PLEDGE

"Honor the Texas Flag.
I pledge allegiance to thee,
Texas, one and indivisible."

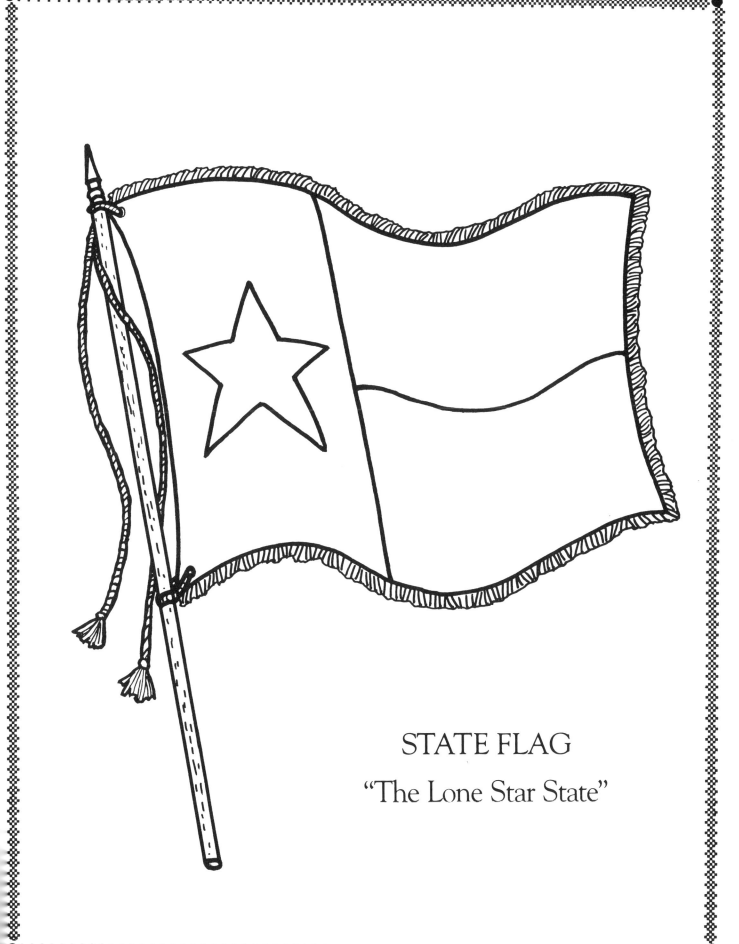

STATE FLAG

"The Lone Star State"

MOCKINGBIRD
State Bird

BLUEBONNET

State Flower

SIDEOATS GRAMA

State Grass

STATE SEAL

Oak leaves: Strength   *Olive leaves: Peace*

PECAN

State Tree

"TEXAS, OUR TEXAS"
State Song

Texas our Texas! all hail the mighty State!
Texas our Texas!
So wonderful so great!
Boldest and grandest, Withstanding ev'ry test;
O Empire wide and glorious, You stand supremely blest.

Texas, O Texas! Your freeborn Single Star,
Sends out its radiance
To nations near and far.
Emblem of Freedom! It sets our hearts aglow,
With thoughts of San Jacinto And glorious Alamo.

Texas, dear Texas! From tyrant grip now free,
Shines forth in splendor
Your Star of Destiny!
Mother of Heroes! We come your children true,
Proclaiming our allegiance Our Faith Our Love for you.

God bless you Texas! And keep you brave and strong,
That you may grow in power and worth, Thro'out the ages
    long.
God bless you Texas! And keep you brave and strong,
That you may grow in power and worth Thro'out the ages
    long.

Reprint permission granted by Mary C Hearne
and Owen Edward Thomas.

STATE CAPITOL
Austin

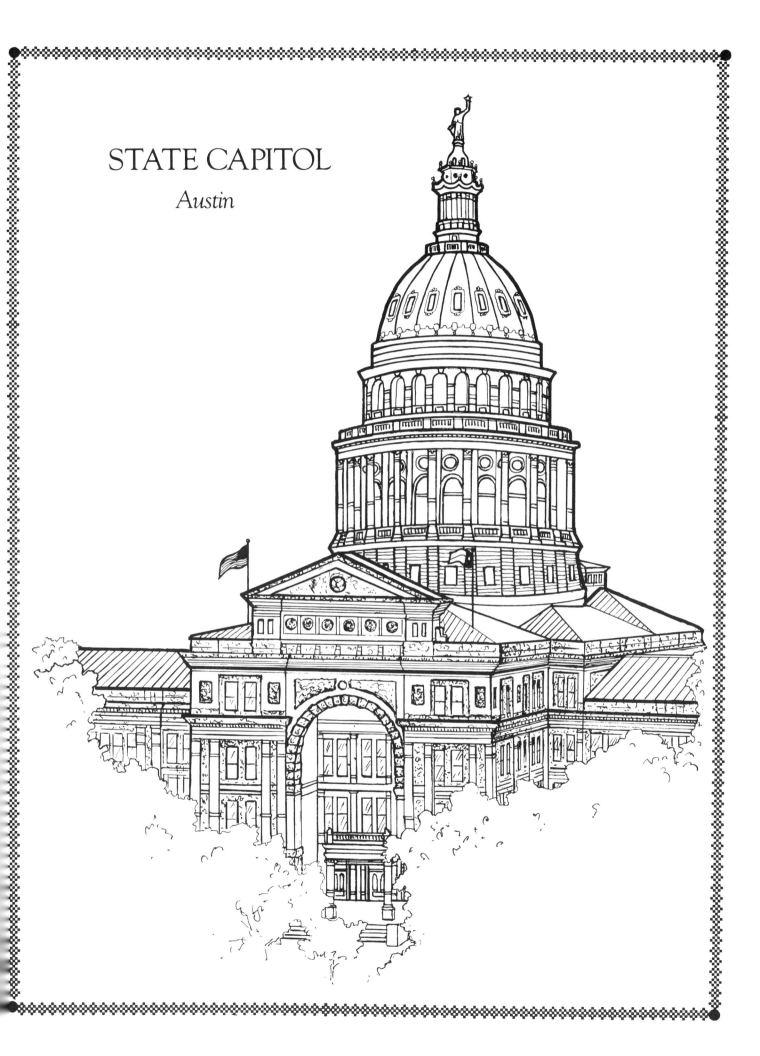

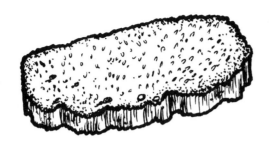

PALMWOOD

State Stone

TOPAZ

State Gem

CHILI

State Dish

FLAGS OVER TEXAS

SPAIN: 1519–1821

FRANCE: 1685, 1690

MEXICO: 1821–1836

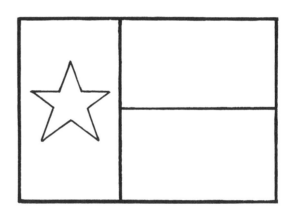

REPUBLIC OF TEXAS: 1836–1846

CONFEDERACY: 1861–1865

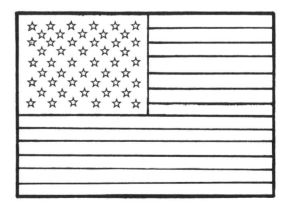

UNITED STATES OF AMERICA:
1846–1861; 1865

TEXAS MAKERS

Stephen F. Austin

Sam Houston

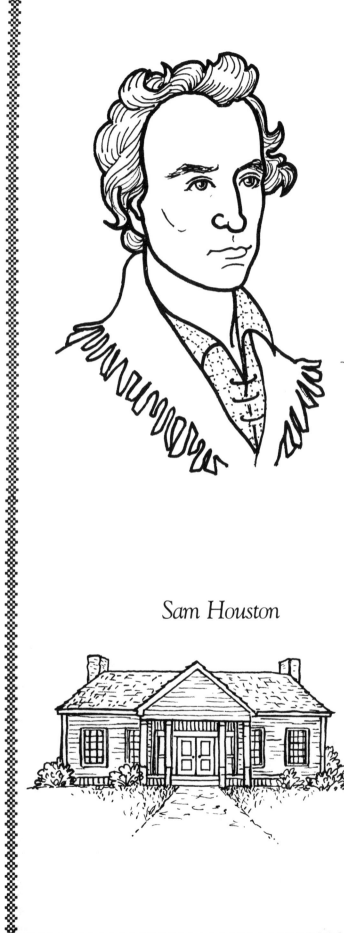

CITRUS FRUITS

WATERMELON

PEACH

ARMADILLO

MONARCH BUTTERFLY

HORNED TOAD

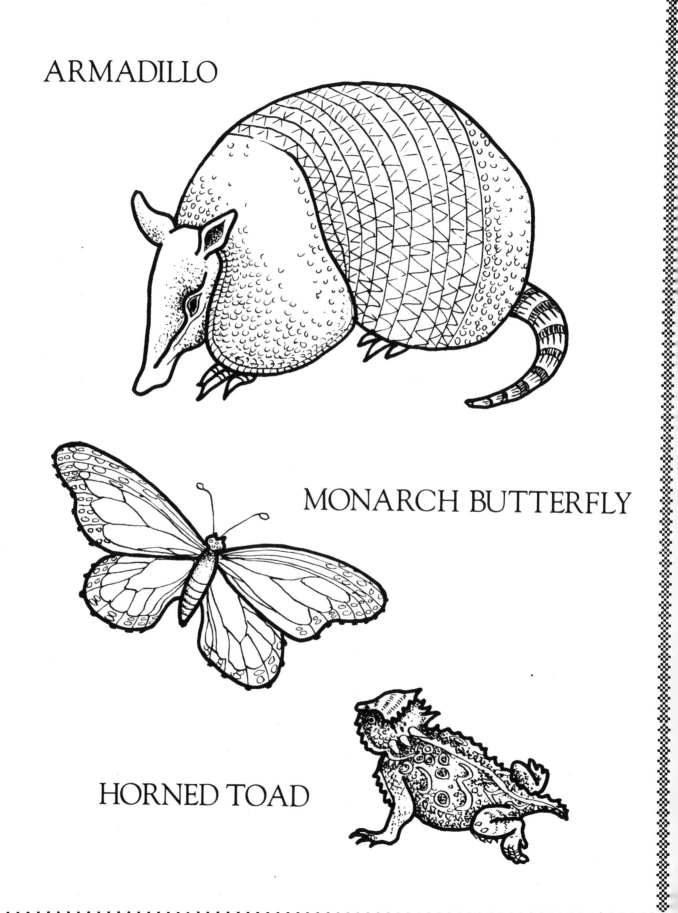

LIGHTHOUSE ROCK
Palo Duro Canyon

PRICKLY PEAR
CACTUS

ROADRUNNER

also called Paisano, Chaparral

COWBOY

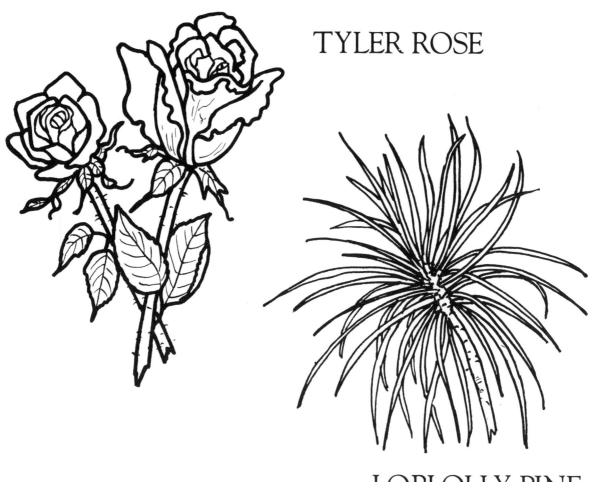

TYLER ROSE

LOBLOLLY PINE

DOGWOOD

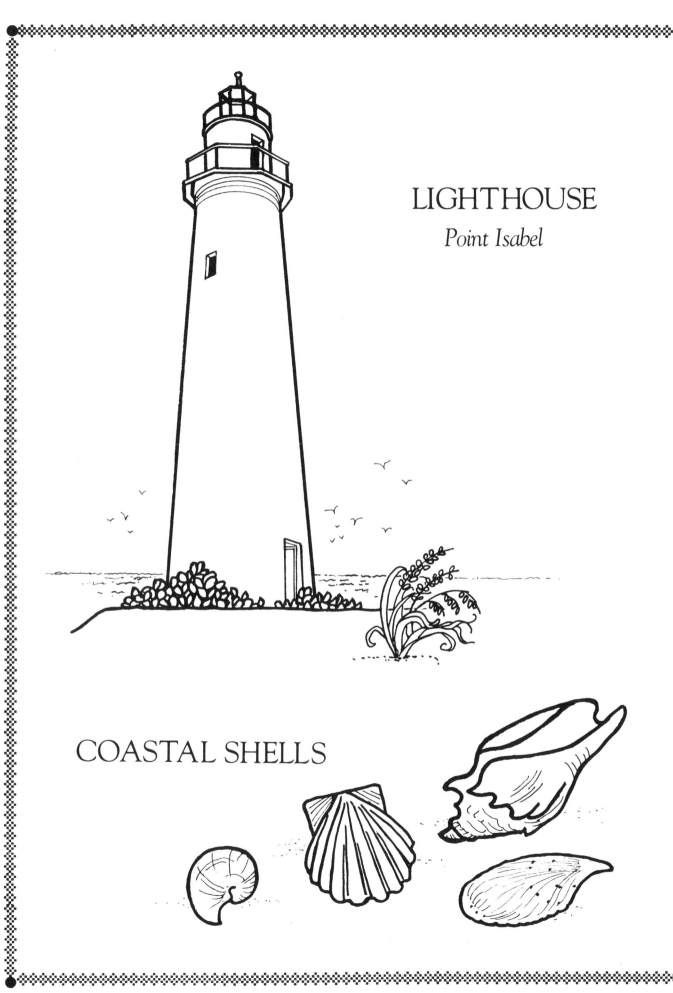

LIGHTHOUSE
Point Isabel

COASTAL SHELLS

LONGHORN

BRANDS

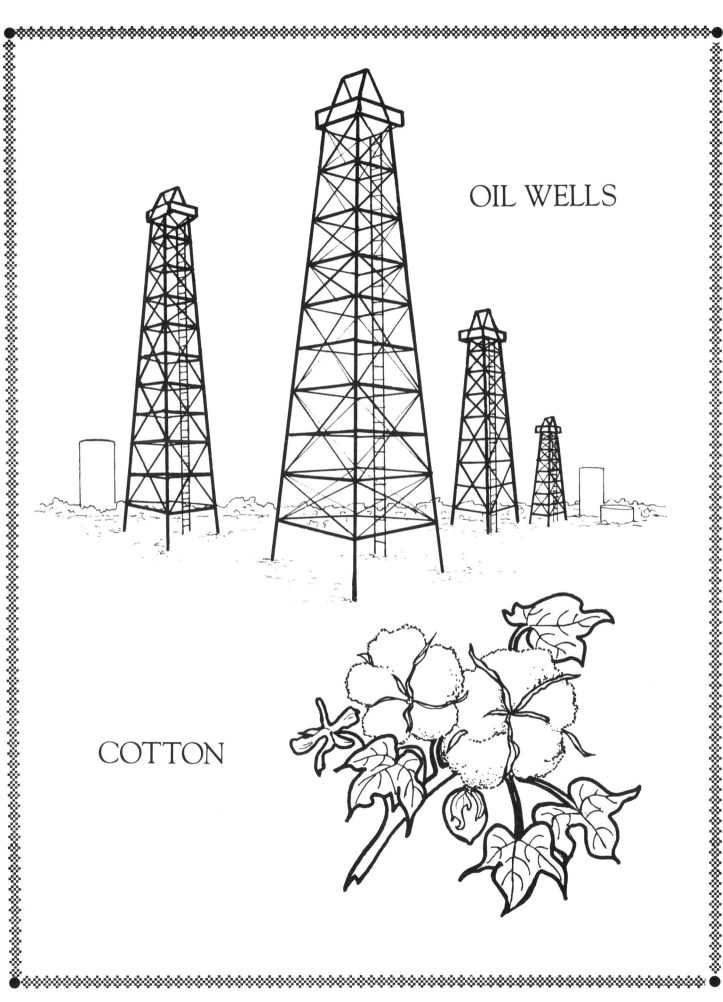

OIL WELLS

COTTON

MISSION SAN JOSÉ

San Antonio

BATTLESHIP TEXAS

near Houston

SAN JACINTO MONUMENT

near Houston

MUSTANG

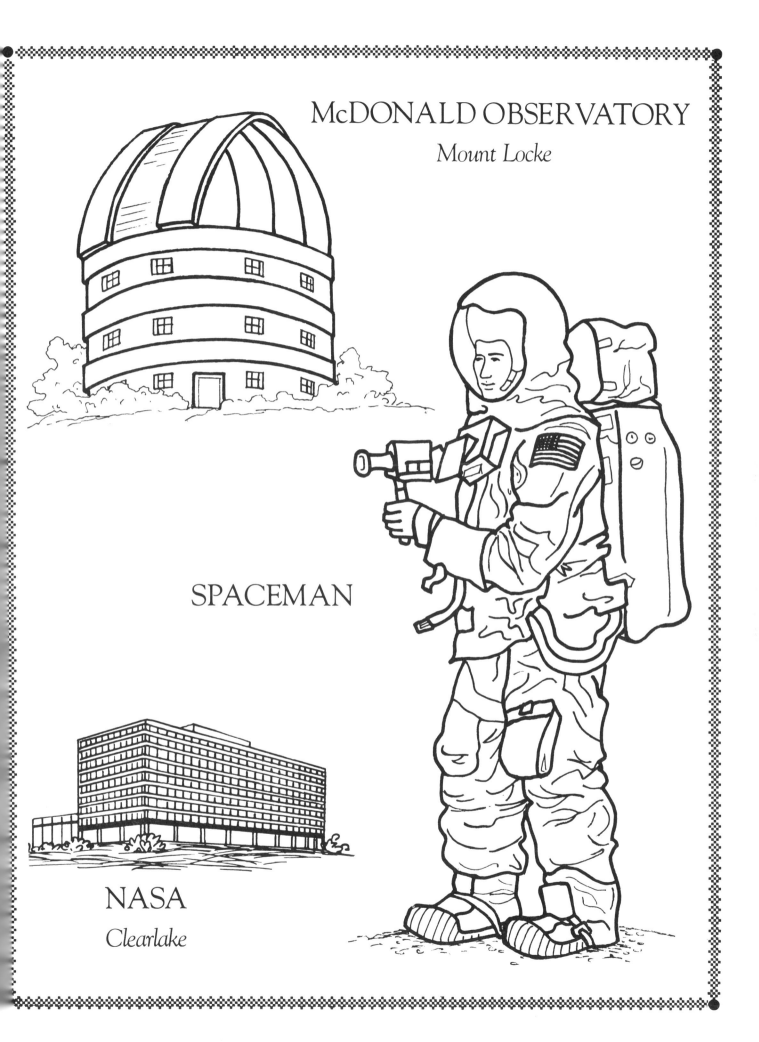

McDONALD OBSERVATORY

Mount Locke

SPACEMAN

NASA

Clearlake

The ALAMO
San Antonio

DEER

COYOTE

JACKRABBIT

RATTLESNAKE

MAP of TEXAS

MAJOR DATES IN TEXAS HISTORY

★ About 10,000 B.C., the first Indians arrived in Texas. These ancient peoples are called Paleo-Indians. They hunted mammoths and giant bison and other animals that later became extinct.

★ After 6,000 B.C., Indian lifeways changed, and archeologists call the time in Texas from then to about A.D. 500 the Archaic Period. During this period Indians painted beautiful murals depicting human scenes and religious ceremonies on cave walls in dry areas of West Texas.

★ The years from A.D. 500 to A.D. 1500 are called the Late Prehistoric Period. Agricultural Indians domesticated some of our principal crops, including cotton, corn, beans, squash, tomatoes, and potatoes. Burial and temple mounds of these early farmers can be found in the piney woods of East Texas.

★ Although six flags have flown over Texas, there have been eight changes of government:

Spanish	1519-1685
French	1685-1690
Spanish	1690-1821
Mexican	1821-1836
Republic of Texas	1836-1845
United States	1845-1861
Confederate States	1861-1865
United States	1865-present

★ In 1519, the Spanish explorer Piñeda made a map of the Texas coast. This event marked the beginning of Spain's rule in Texas.

★ Nine years later, in 1528, Cabeza de Vaca was shipwrecked near Galveston. His small band met many Indian tribes while wandering through the Texas area, but he finally came to a Spanish settlement. He made his way to Mexico City with tales of the fabled "Seven Cities of Gold."

★ In the early 1540s, Coronado, in an attempt to find the seven cities, explored throughout present New Mexico, West Texas, and as far north as Kansas. Though he found no cities of gold, he strengthened Spain's claim on Texas.

★ Corpus Christi de la Isleta, established near El Paso in 1682, was the first Spanish mission and pueblo in Texas.

★ The French claim on Texas rests on La Salle's visit in 1685. He established Fort St. Louis in the Matagorda Bay area. Two years later, he was killed by one of his own men. By 1690, Indians and disease had destroyed the small French force.

★ A Spanish expedition was sent in 1689 to destroy Fort St. Louis; in 1690, the empty fort was discovered. Alarmed by the French presence in Texas and the French settlements in the Louisiana area, the Spaniards established Mission San Francisco de los Tejas, the first East Texas mission.

★ In 1718, with the establishment of Mission San Antonio de Valero (the Alamo), the city of San Antonio was founded.

★ In 1821, the year Mexico gained independence from Spain, Stephen F. Austin received permission from the Mexican government to settle a colony of 300 families, now known as the "Old Three Hundred," in what later became Austin County in southeast Texas. This settlement was the beginning of the Anglo-American colonization in Texas that would bring between 35,000 and 50,000 settlers from the United States by 1836.

★ Early in 1835, Stephen F. Austin announced that he was convinced that war with Mexico was necessary to secure freedom. Growing tension in Texas was the result of cultural, political, and religious differences between the Anglo-Americans and the Mexican government. In response to the unrest, Antonio Lopez de Santa Anna, the president of Mexico, reinforced Mexican troops in Texas. A battle fought at Gonzales on Oct. 2, 1835, in which the Mexican forces were thwarted in their efforts to retrieve a cannon, gave rise to the famous flag bearing the words "Come and Take It." Though there were earlier minor skirmishes, the Battle of Gonzales is generally considered to be the first battle for Texas' independence.

★ The Battle of the Alamo, lasting nearly two weeks, ended on Mar. 6, 1836, with the deaths of all its defenders (numbering about 187). The Mexican army of Santa Anna numbered 4,000 to 5,000 during its final charge. Among those killed were David Crockett, Jim Bowie, and William B. Travis. A subsequent massacre of Texans who had surrendered at Goliad on March 27 led to the battle cry of Texas' independence, "Remember the Alamo! Remember Goliad!"

★ The Texas Declaration of Independence was enacted at Washington-on-the-Brazos on Mar. 2, 1836.

★ The Battle of San Jacinto was fought on Apr. 21, 1836, near the present city of Houston. Santa Anna's entire force of 1,600 men was killed or captured by Gen. Sam Houston's army of 800 Texans; only nine Texans lost their lives. This decisive battle resulted in Texas' independence from Mexico.

★ Sam Houston, a native of Virginia, was president of the Republic of Texas for two separate terms, 1836-38 and 1841-44. He also was governor of the state of Texas from 1859 to 1861.

★ Stephen F. Austin, known as the "Father of Texas," died Dec. 27, 1836, after serving two months as secretary of state for the new Republic.

★ Jose Antonio Navarro, signer of the Texas Declaration of Independence and one of the framers of the Constitution of the Republic, was a Texas native, born in San Antonio in 1795. He also served in the Republic of Texas Congress and the Constitutional Convention of 1845. Navarro County was named in his honor.

★ The first Congress of the Republic of Texas convened October 1836 at Columbia (now West Columbia).

★ In 1836, five sites served as temporary capitals of Texas (Washington-on-the-Brazos, Harrisburg, Galveston, Velasco, and Columbia) before Sam Houston moved the capital to Houston in 1837. In 1840, the capital was moved to the new town of Austin.

★ The *Adelsverein,* organized in 1842 in Germany, assisted in bringing many German immigrants to Texas. The first group arrived in Galveston in 1844 and settled at the present site of New Braunfels.

★ Texas was annexed to the United States as the 28th state on Dec. 29, 1845.

★ Texas seceded from the United States and joined the Confederate States of America on Jan. 28, 1861.

★ Texas officially was readmitted to the Union on Mar. 30, 1870, following the period of Reconstruction.

★ The present Texas Constitution was ratified on Feb. 15, 1876.

★ In 1936, Texas celebrated its centennial. Historical markers, placed by the Centennial Commission, later were the basis for the historical marker program of the Texas Historical Commission.

★ On Nov. 22, 1963, President John F. Kennedy was assassinated during a motorcade through downtown Dallas. Vice-President Lyndon B. Johnson of Texas was sworn in as president aboard the presidential airplane at Dallas' Love Field airport that same day.

DID YOU KNOW?

• Nacogdoches and Ysleta are considered to be the two oldest towns in Texas. Ysleta, originally on the Mexican side of the Rio Grande, became part of Texas following a change in the river's course.

• Texas A&M University opened its doors Oct. 4, 1876, and was the state's first land-grant college.

• The University of Texas held its first class in 1883.

• Although a small group of Texas Rangers had been formed in 1823 by Stephen F. Austin, they were not formally organized until Oct. 17, 1835.

• The Rough Riders, recruited in 1898 as a cavalry outfit, were trained in San Antonio by Leonard Wood and Theodore "Teddy" Roosevelt. They fought in the Spanish-American War to liberate Cuba from Spain.

• Spindletop, near Beaumont in East Texas, was Texas' first oil gusher in 1901. It signaled the beginning of the state's oil boom.

• In 1978, 71 million barrels of oil were produced in Yoakum County. That is an average of 195,000 barrels per day.

• On Sept. 8-9, 1900, an estimated 8,000 people were killed in the disastrous Galveston hurricane and flood.

• The tidewater coastline of Texas stretches 624 miles along the Gulf of Mexico and contains more than 600 historic shipwrecks.

• There are more than 70,000 miles of highways in Texas.

• Texas has a total of 6,300 square miles of in-land lakes and streams, second only to Alaska.

• The tallest point in Texas is Guadalupe Peak at 8,751 feet.

• On Apr. 16, 1947, more than 550 people were killed in a chemical explosion in Texas City.

• Mirabeau B. Lamar, second president of the Republic of Texas (1838-41), is called the "Father of Education in Texas."

• The last president of the Republic of Texas was Anson Jones (1844-46), and the first governor of the state was James Pinckney Henderson (1846-47).

• Miriam A. "Ma" Ferguson was the second woman to serve as governor in the United States, but because of the date of elections in Texas, she was technically the first woman elected to that office. She served from 1925 to 1927 and again from 1933 to 1935.

- Texas has two United States senators and 27 United States representatives.

- The Texas Legislature meets for its regular session in the spring of odd numbered years. The governor may convene a special session for the legislators to address particular issues.

- The bicameral (senate and house of representatives) Texas Legislature consists of 33 senators and 150 representatives.

- The governor of Texas is elected to a four-year term in November of even-numbered, non-presidential election years.

- The Capitol in Austin, built of Texas pink granite, opened May 16, 1888. The dome of the Capitol stands seven feet higher than that of the National Capitol in Washington, D.C.

- Jane Long (1798-1880), known as the "Mother of Texas," was a pioneer Anglo-American woman settler in Texas.

- The Governor's Mansion, built in 1856, is the oldest remaining public building in downtown Austin.

- Many famous Texans, including some former governors, are buried in the State Cemetery in Austin.

- "Blind" Lemon Jefferson (1897-1929), born in Freestone County, rose from street beggar to one of the greatest jazz musicians in the world. Scott Joplin (1869-1917), from Bowie County, is known as the "King of Ragtime Music."

- Texas has 254 counties. Rockwall County (147 square miles) is the smallest, and Brewster County (6,204 square miles) is the largest. Only one, Angelina County, is named for a woman.

- The 1850 census recorded 213,000 people in Texas. In 1900, there were three million people, and by 1980, the population was more than 14 million.

- There are three existing Indian reservations in the state: the Alabama-Coushatta Reservation, located between Livingston and Woodville in East Texas; Ysleta del Sur Pueblo (Tigua Indian Reservation) near El Paso; and the Kickapoo Reservation in Maverick County. Most Native Americans in Texas live outside reservations, however. Texas' Indian population ranks sixth among the states, with approximately 65,000 Indians.

- The largest body of water completely within the boundaries of Texas is Sam Rayburn Reservoir (in East Texas), which covers 113,400 acres.

- Texas has four national forests (Angelina, Davy Crockett, Sabine, and Sam Houston), two national parks (Big Bend and Guadalupe Mountains), one national seashore (Padre Island), one national preserve (the Big Thicket), one national recreation area (Amistad), and numerous national historic sites.

- With more than 267,000 square miles, Texas occupies about seven percent of the total water and land area of the United States. It is 801 miles from the northwest corner of the Panhandle to the southern tip of the state, and 773 miles from the western tip near El Paso to the Sabine River, the eastern boundary of the state.

- Texas is as large as all of New England, New York, Pennsylvania, Ohio, and Illinois combined.

- There are currently more than 11,000 historical markers in the state. Marker subjects include historic courthouses, frontier forts, Spanish missions and presidios, cemeteries, churches, individuals, historic homes and buildings, Texas Revolution battle sites, and more. There are more than 700 local history museums, 40,000 recorded archeological sites, and more than 2,000 sites listed in the National Register of Historic Places in Texas.

- In 1976 a State Department of Highways and Public Transportation survey indicated that nearly 55 percent of the tourists who came to Texas were traveling to visit historic attractions. A 1985 survey by *Southern Living* magazine concluded that 67 percent of its readers traveled primarily to visit historic sites.

- Dr. Annie Webb Blanton (1870-1945) became the first woman to be elected to statewide office in Texas when she won the race for State Superintendent of Public Instruction in 1918. Eight years later Margie Neal (1875-1971) of Carthage was elected Texas' first woman senator.

- Eighty-five percent of the public libraries in Texas were founded by women's clubs.

- During World War II, the headquarters of the Women's Airforce Service Pilots (WASPs) was located at Avenger

Field in Sweetwater. During the same period, the Women's Army Corps (WACs) was led by a Texas woman, Col. Oveta Culp Hobby.

- There were 72 World War II prisoner-of-war camps in Texas, more than in any other state. Primarily housing German soldiers from the famed *Afrika Korps,* the Texas camps also held Italian and Japanese prisoners.

- In the spring of 1554, the *Santa Maria de Yciar,* the *San Esteban,* and the *Espiritu Santo,* three out of four ships of a Spanish treasure fleet laden with colonists and silver, ran aground on the southern coast of Texas. The treasures are on display in the Corpus Christi Museum.

Resources

A free Texas highway map and tourist literature are available by writing: State Department of Highways and Public Transportation, Travel and Information Division, P.O. Box 5064, Austin, TX 78763.

The Texas Almanac is full of history, facts, and statistics. It is published every other year by *The Dallas Morning News* and is available through bookstores.

The *Handbook of Texas* is a three-volume reference source with alphabetical listings of people, places, and historical events. Copies are available in most Texas libraries and bookstores, or you can write: Texas State Historical Association, Sid Richardson Hall 2.306, University of Texas, Austin, TX 78712.

Courtesy Texas Historical Commission

IT'S A FACT

AREA: Texas covers 275,416 square miles (land, inland water, and submerged tidelands to 3 leagues) – large enough to fit 15 of the 50 states within its borders and still have 1,000 square miles left over. Texas extends 801 straight-line miles from north to south and 773 miles from east to west.

BOUNDARY: The boundary of Texas extends 3,816 miles with Louisiana on the east, Arkansas on the northeast, Oklahoma on the north, New Mexico on the west, and Mexico and the Gulf of Mexico on the south. The Rio Grande forms the longest segment of the boundary, 1,248 miles. Second longest segment, 726 miles, is formed by the Red River. The tidewater coastline extends 624 miles.

WEATHER: Characterized by generally mild temperatures, Texas weather ranges from a summer mean of 78° in the Panhandle to 84° in the lower Rio Grande Valley, and from winter means of 40° in the Panhandle to 61° in the Valley. Average annual rainfall varies greatly – from more than 59 inches along the Sabine River (more than New Orleans), to less than 8 inches in extreme West Texas (as little as Phoenix).

TERRAIN: The state's surface ranges from sea level to rocky ramparts looming above a mile high in the mountainous Trans-Pecos region. The southern terminus of the table-flat Great Plains of the United States fills much of the Texas Panhandle. Nearly as flat are vast coastal plains along the entire arc of the Gulf of Mexico. Grassy, rolling prairies, where ranches and Texas cowboys still thrive, cover thousands of square miles. Deep forests blanket millions of East Texas acres. In the Central Texas Hill Country, steep limestone hills enfold secluded valleys. There are sun-baked desert lands, rich, black farm lands, humid swamps where wild orchids grow, and dramatic volcanic intrusions of dark basalt and glistening granite.

MOUNTAINS: Texas has 91 mountains a mile or more high, all of them in the Trans-Pecos region. Guadalupe Peak, at 8,749 feet the state's highest mountain, is more than 2,000 feet higher than North Carolina's Mount Mitchell, greatest elevation east of the Mississippi River. Other mountains are Bush 8,676; Bartlett 8,513; Baldy 8,382; Livermore 8,381; Hunter 8,362, and El Capitan 8,085.

RIVERS: Longest river in the state is the Rio Grande, which forms the international boundary between Texas and Mexico and extends 1,248 miles along Texas. Next longest river running through Texas or along its boundary line is the Red. The Brazos is the longest river between the Rio Grande and the Red. Other principal rivers are the Colorado, Trinity, Sabine, Nueces, Neches, Pecos and Guadalupe.

CAPITOL: The nation's largest state capitol, in Austin, was completed in 1888. Built of Texas pink granite, it was paid for by deeding three million acres of public land to a firm of Chicago businessmen. Within some 8.5 acres of floor space are nearly 500 rooms. The building is 309 feet tall from the basement floor to the top of the statue on the dome.

Courtesy Travel & Information Division
State Department of Highways & Public Transportation
Consult a public or school library for more information on Texas.